GIRLS PLAY TOO

For Evanna and all the other girls who thought that boys were better. Always remember, girls play too.

Jacqui Hurley is one of Ireland's leading sports broadcasters. She represented Ireland at basketball and also played camogie for Cork. In 2009, she became the first ever female anchor of *Sunday Sport* on RTÉ Radio One. She now anchors RTÉ's rugby coverage on television and *The Sunday Game*. She has presented all of the major sporting events, including the Olympics, World Cups, the Euros & multiple All-Ireland finals. She lives in Dublin with her husband Shane and her children, Luke and Lily.

Jacqui Hurley

Jacqui Hurley

GIRLS PLAY TOO

INSPIRING STORIES OF IRISH SPORTSWOMEN

MERRION
PRESS

First published in hardback in 2020 by
Merrion Press
10 George's Street
Newbridge
Co. Kildare
Ireland
www.merrionpress.ie

This paperback edition published 2023

9781785374661 (Paper)
9781785373381 (Kindle)
9781785373398 (Epub)

A CIP catalogue record for this book is
available from the British Library.

Cover design and typesetting by **riverdesignbooks.com**
Cover illustrations by **Jennifer Farley**

Merrion Press is a member of Publishing Ireland.

CONTENTS

ACKNOWLEDGEMENTS

IT'S BEEN A LONG JOURNEY TO GET THIS BOOK TO THE SHELVES – THANK YOU TO THE MANY PEOPLE WHO HAVE HELPED TO MAKE THAT HAPPEN.

To the athletes, for giving me your time and allowing me to share your stories. I hope you know you are inspiring a new generation.

To our five amazing illustrators, who worked together and made this such a unique and special book, celebrating Irish female talent in so many ways.

To Patrick O'Donoghue, for your unwavering support – from taking a phone call out of the blue, to making this ambitious project come to life. I'll be forever grateful you took the chance. To Conor Graham, Maeve Convery and Grace Milusich at Merrion Press, thanks for believing in the project and taking it on.

And a special thanks to the team at River Design, Latte and Melanie Goldstein, who did such an amazing job with the design.

To my early proofreaders, Emma and Cassandra Manning – Emma if you ever play for Dublin I'll pay you back by making an exception and cheering for the Dubs!

To my friends and colleagues for all your advice and support: Elaine Buckley, Evanne Ní Chuilinn, Marie Crowe, Paul O'Flynn, Damian Lawlor, Paul McDermott, Nora Stapleton, Mary O'Connor, Sharon O'Connor and Sarah Colgan. It takes a village!

To Joe Mooney, Sarah Gordon, Sian Gray and Dylan Smith at Lidl, for backing this book and for always keeping women in sport on the main agenda.

Finally, to my family. I was lucky to grow up in a house where sport was equal and for everyone, and I'm so glad my children now have that too. Thank you Shane, for making sure Lily does as many push ups as Luke! It's a battle out there and I'm glad you're on her side!

ABOUT THIS BOOK

When I was a young girl, Sonia O'Sullivan was my sporting idol. I loved the idea that a girl from Cork could become a world champion and she inspired a generation of children to think that maybe we could do it too.

Everyone in Ireland knew who Sonia was because she was a global superstar, but also because you could watch her races on tv and read about her in newspapers. What I didn't understand at the time, was that this was a rare privilege for an Irish female athlete. So many more of them battled bravely in the background, with very little attention on them.

Thankfully, over the years, this has started to change. There are more opportunities for girls, there is more female sport being televised, written about and talked about than ever before, and a whole new generation of Irish girls are getting to witness new heroes being created.

I wrote this book so you can learn more about those heroes — not superheroes in capes, but ones who wear football boots, boxing gloves and mouth guards. I want you to read about fairytales that aren't about princesses in a castle and mostly, I want you to know that some fairytales start in your back garden and end up with an Olympic or an All-Ireland medal.

I hope the stories of the twenty-five athletes in this book will give you the inspiration to see that if you work hard enough anything is possible, even if you're a girl.

Who knows, maybe someday you could be the sporting hero that people look up to, just like the girls in this book!

★ LEGENDS OF

Maeve Kyle ★ Athletics

In 1956, Maeve Kyle became Ireland's first female Olympian, when she competed in the 100m and 200m races at the Melbourne Olympics. At the time, some people considered it dangerous for women to run, but Maeve held strong and campaigned for women's rights. She was also a talented hockey player and won fifty-eight caps for Ireland.

Rosemary Smith ★ Motorsport

Rosemary Smith was the queen of motorsport in the 1960s and 1970s. She became the first, and only, woman to win the Dutch 'Tulip Rally' in 1965 and famously broke the land speed record in 1978. Just a few years ago, Rosemary broke another record, becoming the oldest person to drive a Formula One car, at seventy-nine years of age.

Jessica Harrington ★ Eventing

Jessica Harrington was one of Ireland's top three-day eventers and represented Ireland at the 1984 Olympics. She had a knack for understanding horses, so after she stopped riding, she took out a trainer's licence. There were very few women involved in racing, so Jessica had to work hard to prove herself. Today, she is one of Ireland's leading trainers.

IRISH SPORT ★

Sonia O'Sullivan ★ Athletics

Sonia O'Sullivan is Ireland's most successful athlete of all time. She won thirteen major medals, including a World Championship medal in 1995, two cross-country world titles, three European Championship medals and a silver medal at the Sydney Olympics in 2000.

Angela Downey ★ Camogie

Angela Downey was only thirteen when she was called up to the senior Kilkenny camogie panel. She played with her county for twenty-four years and won twelve All-Ireland titles between 1974 and 1994. She is widely regarded as the greatest player to have ever played the game.

Deirdre Gogarty ★ Boxing

Deirdre Gogarty was Ireland's first female world boxing champion. She fought at a time when boxing was illegal for women in Ireland, so she had to go abroad for fights. Her fight against Christy Martin in 1996 was seen by over thirty million viewers on pay-per-view. Deirdre paved the way for so many Irish female boxers, including Katie Taylor and Kellie Harrington.

KATIE TAYLOR

BOXING

Once there was a girl called Katie, and all she ever wanted to be was an Olympic champion. She tried lots of other sports and even played soccer for Ireland. But boxing was her true passion and nothing would get in the way of that.

When Katie started boxing, girls weren't allowed to fight in competitions, so she had to pretend to be a boy to enter. She would hide her ponytail under her headgear and stay in her dressing room until the last minute, in case someone saw her and realised she was a girl. It was only after she had beaten the boys, that she would take off her headgear and show them who she really was.

Katie campaigned for girls to be allowed to fight in Ireland and she won that battle too! Pretty soon, she wasn't just a big star in Ireland, she was winning European and World titles.

Boxing wasn't always an Olympic sport for women, but when the judges saw Katie fight, they agreed the world had to see her box on the biggest stage. So they introduced it for the first time at the London Olympics in 2012.

As Katie started her ring walk for the gold medal fight, she knew her life was about to change. After one of the toughest fights of her career, the referee lifted Katie's hand and she fell to her knees; she had fulfilled her childhood dream of becoming an Olympic champion.

Having conquered all she could in the amateur game – an Olympic gold medal, five World titles and six European titles – Katie turned professional in 2016. Within three years, she won every belt possible, to become the undisputed lightweight champion of the world. Katie was involved in the biggest women's boxing match in history, when she beat Amanda Serrano in front of a sell-out crowd at Madison Square Garden in 2022. It was the first ever female fight to headline the iconic venue and Katie's memorable win cemented her place as the greatest female fighter the world has ever seen.

RENA BUCKLEY

CAMOGIE & LADIES FOOTBALL

Once there was a girl called Rena, who loved playing matches in the backyard with her brother and sister. Rena would pretend she was Cork hurling and football star Teddy McCarthy, who won four All-Ireland medals. All Rena dreamed about was doing the same.

Rena loved the GAA and she loved the Irish language. After matches at home, she would climb the back steps and pretend to accept the cup, always making her winning speech in Irish.

When the Cork camogie team won the All-Ireland in 1995 and 1997, they brought the O'Duffy Cup to Rena's club, Inniscarra. Rena knew that it would take a lot of hard work if she wanted to bring the cup back herself someday. So she trained every single day and was never seen without a hurley or a football in her hand.

Rena began her Cork career playing with the u14s and within a year she was called up to the senior football panel. She was on the senior camogie panel by the time she was seventeen.

Rena had just turned eighteen when she won her first All-Ireland with the Cork camogie team in 2005. Two weeks later, she won her second with the Cork footballers. Rena couldn't believe it. All she dreamed about was winning an All-Ireland and suddenly she had two in a fortnight! But it wasn't always easy playing the two sports. One day Rena even had to play camogie for Cork in the morning and football for Cork in the evening, travelling a few hundred miles between the two matches.

On those journeys, Rena often thought about those speeches she practised in her backyard. So in 2012, when she was captain of the footballers, she decided she would say her entire winning speech in Irish. Five years later she did it again, when she captained the camogie team to victory.

That win was Rena's last ever game for Cork. She retired as the most successful player in the history of the GAA, with eighteen All-Ireland medals – eleven in football and seven in camogie.

Rena Buckley

RACHAEL BLACKMORE

HORSE RACING

Once there was a girl called Rachael, who was always adventurous. She climbed out of her cot before her first birthday and has been jumping over obstacles ever since!

Rachael grew up on a farm in Tipperary, surrounded by animals. She had her own pony called Bubbles, who would take her on little adventures around the farm. Even in her wildest dreams, Rachael never imagined she could be a champion jockey. It wasn't seen as a professional career for women and it never dawned on Rachael that she might be the one to help change that.

Rachael won her first pony race in Cork when she was thirteen years old. She loved the thrill of winning and decided that horse racing was the next step, so she started riding out for a local horse trainer when she was in transition year. She rode as an amateur while she was in college and even missed her graduation in the University of Limerick because she was racing, much to her mother's disappointment!

After four successful years as an amateur, Rachael decided to turn professional in 2015. In doing so, she became the first female professional jockey in Ireland since the 1980s.

It was a brave move and even though she was racing full-time against mostly men, Rachael never thought she was any different – she just wanted to win. Every jockey dreams of winning a race at the Cheltenham Festival and in March 2019 Rachael rode her first two winners at the famous event. But not even Rachael could have dreamed of the success that would follow soon afterwards.

In 2021, she became the first ever woman to be crowned champion jockey at Cheltenham, after riding six winners over the four days. Just a few weeks later she won the Grand National, the most famous race in the world. She won the Cheltenham Gold Cup the following year, completing a trio of memorable victories. Rachael never set out to be the first woman to achieve these things, but her victories will inspire so many more girls to chase dreams that once seemed impossible, just like she did.

Rachael Blackmore

FIONA COGHLAN

RUGBY

Once there was a girl called Fiona, who was obsessed with horse riding and tennis. Every summer Fiona and her friends would make their own tennis court and play 'Wimbledon' on the road. There was only one rule – Fiona had to be Steffi Graf!

Fiona never played rugby when she was younger; it wasn't really played by girls, because some people thought it was too rough for them! She didn't actually play team sports until she was in secondary school and it was even later when she started playing rugby, taking it up in college after a friend suggested she give it a try.

Within one year, Fiona went from watching the Irish women in action to playing with them in the Six Nations. The early days were difficult, with some embarrassing results, including a 79–0 defeat by England. Very little money was spent on the team and on away weekends they often had to sleep on the same gym floor that they had trained on that day. There was even one game where the team had to take an overnight train through France, travel for twenty-seven hours and then play a Six Nations game, after just three hours' sleep!

Fiona became one of the team's key leaders in helping to bring about a change in the women's game and her talent and commitment was recognised when she was named Ireland captain. Ten years after playing for Ireland for the first time, Fiona got her big reward, leading Ireland to a first ever Grand Slam (beating England, France, Italy, Scotland and Wales) in 2013. The final match against Italy was the first ever women's rugby international to be shown live on RTÉ television and it drew a huge audience to the women's game.

At the World Cup the following year, they became the first Irish rugby team to beat New Zealand – a famous win that kick-started a new revolution in Irish women's rugby.

Fiona Coghlan

DENISE O'SULLIVAN

SOCCER

Once there was a girl called Denise, who was told she was too small to play soccer. At trials for the u15 Munster schools' team, the coaches told her parents she had lots of talent but, due to her size, she would never make it to the top level of the sport. Denise was heartbroken but her mum and dad knew she was good enough, so they convinced her to go back to the trials the following year and prove the coaches wrong. It was the best decision she ever made! Not only did she make the team but Munster won the tournament, and soon afterwards Denise was picked to play for the Irish schools' team.

Denise's rise through the ranks with the Republic of Ireland happened very quickly. One year she was winning a silver medal with the u17s at the European Championships and reaching the quarter-finals of the u17 World Cup, and the next year she scored two goals for the senior team in a dream debut against Wales. Suddenly, Denise had the football world at her feet.

The only problem was Denise really didn't want to leave her family. When phone calls came from football managers trying to offer her a professional contract, she would pretend she wasn't home! Eventually, her family convinced her to take a chance on Glasgow City in 2013 and so began a career that would take Denise all over the world.

In the space of one week in 2016, Denise's life changed in so many ways. Just as she signed a deal to play football in America, in the biggest women's league on the planet, her dad died of cancer. It was even harder to leave her family this time, but Denise knew it was what her dad would have wanted.

Within a few years Denise was voted MVP (Most Valuable Player) by her teammates, as she helped North Carolina Courage to league titles in 2018 and 2019. Denise's life long dream was to play for Ireland at a major tournament and in 2022 that dream came true, as Ireland qualified for the World Cup for the very first time. From a small girl on the streets of Knocknaheeny in Cork, she had become one of the top footballers in the world.

SUSAN MORAN

BASKETBALL

Once there was a girl called Susan, who was really good at tennis. She represented Ireland at underage level, but her parents knew that taking the next step and playing abroad would mean Susan leaving school, and they didn't want her to do that.

Luckily, Susan's PE teacher started a school basketball team and convinced Susan to try that instead. Within a few years, Susan led her school and club in Tullamore to an All-Ireland double win, scoring forty-eight points in one game and fifty-two points in the other.

News of Susan's talents had spread around the country and she was picked for the Irish senior women's team when she was only sixteen. A basketball scout from St Joseph's University in Philadelphia travelled to watch her play and offered her a scholarship to go to college in America. Even though it was far from home, Susan knew it was a huge opportunity and she was determined to take it.

Susan made an immediate impact in America. She was small for her position but she worked really hard and the coaches made her a starter on the team in her first year. Susan went on to start every single game of her four-year college career and she became the team's all-time leading scorer. When Susan left St Joseph's University, they retired her number 10 jersey and inducted her into the Hall of Fame.

Playing professionally was Susan's dream, and in 2002, she became the first – and only – Irish woman to play in the WNBA (Women's National Basketball Association), when she joined the New York Liberty. Susan's basketball career took her all over the world, playing professionally in Spain, Australia and New Zealand.

She now works as a coach with St Joseph's University, where she walks onto the same basketball court she played on and wonders if someday she can help one of her players to break her scoring records!

Susan Moran #10

LEONA MAGUIRE

Once there was a girl called Leona, who had a twin sister called Lisa, and they did everything together. When they were nine years old, Lisa broke her elbow and the doctor suggested a swinging-action sport might help to rebuild the muscle. Leona didn't want Lisa to have to do the recovery alone, so they both took up golf and it quickly became their favourite sport.

Leona and Lisa were so used to competing against each other, that competing against other people was often easier. By the time they were eleven, Lisa was the world u12 champion and Leona finished third. Two years later, Leona won the Irish Senior Ladies Close Championship for the first time, beating Lisa in the final.

In 2010, Leona and Lisa were chosen to play in the famous Curtis Cup, the biggest team trophy for female amateur golfers. The only problem was, playing would mean missing their Junior Cert exams. Luckily their school principal understood how important playing was to them and he let them use their mock exams as their Junior Certs, so they wouldn't miss out on such a huge opportunity.

After secondary school, Leona and Lisa went to America on golf scholarships. Leona made such a big impact that, after just a few months, she was ranked the number one amateur golfer in the world. Her record of 135 weeks in a row as number one is the longest run in history.

The twins achieved a lifelong dream of turning professional in 2018, and while Lisa had to make the difficult decision to retire after a year on tour, Leona's game went from strength to strength. In 2021, Leona played a starring role for Team Europe in the prestigious Solheim Cup, as they narrowly beat Team USA 15–13. Leona's remarkable performance saw her break the all-time rookie record with four and a half points out of a possible five.

The following year Leona claimed her first win on the LPGA Tour (Ladies Professional Golf Association) at the Drive On Championship in Florida, becoming the first ever Irish winner in the tour's history.

★ ★ ★ 16 ★ ★ ★   *Leona Maguire*

LINDSAY PEAT

BASKETBALL, LADIES FOOTBALL & RUGBY

Once there was a girl called Lindsay, who scored five goals in a Cumann na mBunscol football final when she was in fifth class, and her team still lost the match. Lindsay was so devastated by the loss that she didn't play Gaelic football again until she was in her twenties.

Instead, Lindsay focused on soccer and basketball and was picked for the Irish team in both sports. Lindsay had lots of natural talent but she struggled with her weight. She knew if she wanted to become a better athlete, she would have to lose some weight, so she worked really hard and in the space of one year she lost five stone!

It all paid off for Lindsay when she was asked to be captain of the Irish basketball team. She also rediscovered her love for football and became a key player for the Dublin footballers. But balancing both sports was not easy. One day in 2009, she played a senior international basketball match for Ireland in the afternoon and was then flown by helicopter to play in an All-Ireland football quarter-final against Kerry that evening! Dublin got to the All-Ireland final that year and lost to Cork, but a year later Lindsay was one of the heroes as Dublin won their first ever ladies' football All-Ireland.

Despite all of her success, Lindsay still wanted one more challenge, so her friend suggested she give rugby a try. She impressed the coaches so much that she was called up to the Irish team within a few months. She made her debut against England in what was only her eighth ever rugby match and while it took her some time to learn the rules, her athletic ability set her apart once again.

Just like she did in every other team she was involved with, Lindsay became a real leader in the Irish rugby squad. Her teammates gave her a standing ovation when she was named Ireland's Player of the Year in 2017, just two years after making her international debut.

SANITA PUSPURE

ROWING

Once there was a girl called Sanita, who grew up in Latvia and was fascinated by boats and the way they moved through the water. She spent a lot of time training and learning the movements before she finally sat in a boat at the age of sixteen. Once she got on the water, she was hooked.

Rowing wasn't a very big sport in Latvia, so even though Sanita was very good, she wasn't getting much recognition for the progress she was making. But when she won a bronze medal at the 1999 European Junior Championships, her mother encouraged her to keep going.

While she was winning lots of races, Sanita still lacked self-confidence. She never thought she was the best racer and always found it hard to enjoy the moment when she won. She loved the training, but she found the big races stressful and eventually she decided to quit rowing.

Sanita moved to Ireland in 2006 and one day she was driving in Dublin with her husband Kasper and their son Patrick, when they took a wrong turn and ended up in Islandbridge near the River Liffey. As they looked around to see where they were going, Sanita spotted some rowing boats. She took this as a sign that maybe her rowing career wasn't finished yet.

Sanita was pregnant at the time but after she had her daughter, Daniela, she joined a rowing club and within a year she was the national champion.

Competing this time around felt so different. With two children, her thoughts on life and her attitude towards training changed. Squeezing two sessions in between school dropoffs and pickups was a challenge, but all the hard work and sacrifice paid off in 2018, when Sanita became world champion. Her family were in the stands a year later when she struck gold once again at the World Rowing Championships. As she stood on the podium, Sanita smiled to herself — taking that wrong turn in 2006 was the best mistake she ever made!

Sanita Puspure

CORA STAUNTON

LADIES FOOTBALL & AUSSIE RULES

Once there was a girl called Cora, who was so good at Gaelic football she was picked for the Mayo ladies senior football team when she was only thirteen.

Cora started playing football with the boys when she was seven years old. At first they didn't want to pass to the girl, but when they saw how good she was they changed their minds – even at that stage, she was better than most of the boys her age!

Cora's breakthrough to the senior team in Mayo was rapid and she was preparing for her first All-Ireland final in 1999 when she broke her collarbone in training. Cora was devastated because she knew she wouldn't be able to play in the final.

Mayo won the All-Ireland that day and Cora helped them to win three more over the next four years, becoming one of the biggest stars in the game. Teams would often put three people marking her and she still scored an average of ten points per game! When she finished playing Gaelic football, she was the all-time leading championship scorer, with 59 goals and 476 points, a record that is unlikely to ever be beaten.

But just as Cora's football career was coming to an end, she was offered the chance to play Aussie Rules. So at thirty-five years of age, she embarked on a new journey to Australia as a professional athlete, becoming the first ever overseas player to be drafted into the AFLW (Australian Football League Women's).

Even though she had to adapt to playing with a different-shaped ball, Cora's natural ability was obvious and she quickly became one of her team's leading scorers.

In 2019, Cora broke her leg in four places – a horrendous injury which threatened to end her career. But somehow Cora battled back, playing on for three more seasons. When she retired in 2023, she finished her AFLW career as the club's all-time leading goal scorer with 55 goals and was recognised as one of the game's best ever players.

OLIVE LOUGHNANE

RACE WALKING

Once there was a girl called Olive, who was so small, her parents found it hard to get a communion dress to fit her. Despite her size, Olive was never afraid to stand up for herself. At her primary school, the boys were encouraged to play sport but the girls were kept inside to do knitting. One day Olive threw down the knitting needles and demanded that the girls be let outside to play too. After that day, the girls never had to stay inside again.

Olive loved the outdoors and first started race walking when she was fifteen. When the national coaches saw her, they knew she had raw talent but Olive wasn't doing any serious training.

While the 1996 Atlanta Olympics were on, Olive met a trainer who told her that, with a lot of hard work, she could be at the next Olympics. Olive thought about it and decided that maybe he was right. Four years later, she competed in her first Olympic Games in Sydney.

When Olive finished seventh in the 20km walk at the 2008 Olympics, she knew she was getting closer to winning her first major medal. Unfortunately, she also knew there were some athletes in her sport who were cheating by taking performance-enhancing drugs. Olive did her best to speak out, but she always told herself, 'Whatever happens, just do *your* best.'

In 2009, Olive had the best race of her life at the World Championships in Berlin. She gave it everything she had and finished second behind a Russian athlete. Olive always suspected the Russian was cheating and eventually she was proved right. Six years later, the Russian athlete was stripped of her medal and disqualified from the race.

Olive couldn't believe it – she never gave up hope that someday the cheaters would be caught, but the reality took some time to sink in. The gold medal from that day in Berlin was now going to be hers. After years of waiting, Olive was finally presented with her gold medal in 2016 – becoming world champion was worth the wait!

Jen Murphy
Sketches

ELLEN KEANE

PARALYMPIC SWIMMING

Once there was a girl called Ellen, who was born without the lower part of her left arm. This made Ellen look different to other girls but she never felt different. She called it her lucky fin!

It was only as Ellen got older that she noticed people would sometimes stare at her, so she started wearing long sleeves to hide her arm. Ellen's Dad knew the only place she felt really comfortable was in the swimming pool, so he entered her in a disability swimming competition in Lisburn, when she was seven years old. When she came home with six medals, they both knew Ellen had found her passion.

Ellen represented Ireland for the first time when she was just nine years old, winning four silver medals at a junior competition. By the time she was eleven, she was training five mornings a week before school.

One day, while she was training for the Paralympics in 2008, Ellen suddenly got a sharp pain in her side. She was rushed to hospital and they realised that she had burst her appendix. She couldn't train for three weeks and she was heartbroken to think she might have to wait four more years to become a Paralympian. Thankfully, Ellen recovered quickly and made history at the Beijing Paralympics, as Ireland's youngest ever competitor at thirteen years of age.

Even though she had achieved her dream of becoming a Paralympian, Ellen was still hiding her arm and it was impacting her training. So, after a difficult Paralympics in London in 2012, she decided it was time for the world to see the real Ellen. She removed the sleeves from her tops and said 'let people stare'.

With her new attitude, life changed for Ellen when she won a bronze medal at the Paralympics in Rio in 2016. Five years later, she set her sights on gold at the Paralympics in Tokyo. After the race of her life, Ellen's hand was first to touch the wall — she was a Paralympic champion. Instead of hiding her arm, Ellen used her profile to change the thinking around disabilities, asking people to 'be the person you needed when you were younger'.

KELLIE HARRINGTON

BOXING

Once there was a girl called Kellie, who was always getting into trouble. She never did her homework and was sent for detention after school nearly every day. By the time she was fourteen, Kellie had left school, deciding it just wasn't for her.

Kellie knew she needed discipline and she thought maybe boxing would be good for her. But no club would take her. They told her 'girls don't box'. Kellie kept going back and eventually, when she was sixteen, Corinthians Boxing Club in Dublin took a chance on her.

Coaches could see Kellie had talent, but she had no self-confidence. It was only when she won a silver medal at the World Championships in 2016 that Kellie really started believing in herself.

One day Kellie was reading and found a quote, 'Tough times never last, but tough people do.' Kellie knew she was tough and decided it was time to prove it to herself and to everyone else. She changed her whole lifestyle and trained every single day. When she went back to the World Championships two years later, Kellie was a different boxer. The lightweight gold medal final was one of the toughest fights of Kellie's career, but when the referee raised her right arm, she knew she had earned the right to be crowned world champion.

Kellie never dreamed of going to the Olympics, but as the Tokyo Games drew closer, she knew she was good enough to win gold. As the outbreak of COVID-19 prevented any of her family from travelling, Kellie fought in empty boxing arenas, but as she advanced through each round her motto became 'hakuna matata' – a line from *The Lion King* that means 'no worries'. Not even breaking her thumb in the year before qualifying for the Olympics or a global pandemic could stop her achieving her destiny.

She knew an Olympic gold medal wouldn't define her, but as she stood on the podium, with a gold medal around her neck, she cried tears of joy. Against all odds, Kellie turned her life around to become a world and Olympic champion.

Kellie Harrington

STEPHANIE ROCHE

Once there was a girl called Stephanie, who grew up playing football with the boys in her estate in Shankill, Dublin. They painted goalposts on the brick walls and from the moment the sun rose until it went down, they were out kicking the ball on the road. Stephanie loved practising new tricks – her favourite one was kicking the ball off the kerb, then smashing it into the goal at the other end.

When Stephanie was thirteen, her Dad took her to join a local girls team in Cabinteely and it wasn't long before she was standing out. The manager of the Irish senior team was at one game where Stephanie's team had lost the match. He came over to Stephanie afterwards and said, 'Unlucky today, but you were brilliant. Keep going and you'll play for Ireland one day.'

Stephanie had never dreamed of playing for Ireland, but from that day it became her main focus. Less than ten years later, the same manager gave Stephanie her first cap for the Republic of Ireland.

In 2013, Stephanie was playing with her club Peamount in the Women's National League when she scored a brilliant goal that quickly went viral on social media. All those hours practising tricks came into her mind as the ball was crossed in to her. She controlled the ball, flicked it over a player's head and smashed it into the net, just like she did on the street as a child. Only this time, millions of people saw it!

Stephanie's goal was nominated for the FIFA Goal of the Year and she was invited to the awards ceremony, alongside some of football's biggest stars, like Lionel Messi and Cristiano Ronaldo. Her goal finished second, in a worldwide vote, behind Real Madrid's James Rodríguez.

Stephanie's life changed after scoring that goal. She was lucky it was caught on film, but she took every opportunity that came her way afterwards, including a chance to become a professional footballer and play in leagues in America, England, France and Italy.

JENNY EGAN

CANOEING

Once there was a girl called Jenny, who was in a canoe before she was even born. Jenny's mum paddled while she was pregnant and it must have rubbed off on Jenny, because from the moment she was born, she loved canoeing too.

Jenny had her first race when she was only eight years old. She was in a four-person canoe with three older girls, who were all fourteen. Jenny was so small she had to wear her mother's life jacket and the other girls laughed at her because she could hardly see over it. But even then Jenny's talent was obvious and by the time she was fourteen, Jenny was both the British National Sprint and Marathon champion.

All through school Jenny represented Ireland, balancing her schoolwork with her training. Although some people thought it wasn't cool for girls to lift weights or go to the gym, Jenny knew that to be the best she had to work hard and gain more muscle. Some classmates even told her she should give up the canoeing for her Leaving Cert year and focus on her studies. Instead, Jenny trained every day before and after school and then went home to do her homework. That year, she won a bronze medal in the Junior Marathon World Championships and still managed to get a better Leaving Cert than some of those who told her to stop canoeing!

In 2018, Jenny won a bronze medal in the World Championships. After a bad start, she was losing ground on the leaders. But Jenny told herself she couldn't give up. She thought of all those extra hours where she pushed herself in the gym. As others tired, Jenny kept going, crossing the line to win Ireland's first ever medal at the Canoe Sprint World Championships.

A lifetime of work went into winning that medal and two more world championship medals soon followed, as she claimed silver in 2021 and bronze once more in 2022. It was Jenny's belief in herself that made her so strong. That belief helped her to a world number one ranking and cemented her place as Ireland's most successful sprint canoeist.

KATIE MULLAN

HOCKEY

Once there was a girl called Katie, who grew up playing with the boys in Derry. It started with her two older brothers in the backyard, then it was with the u14 boys hurling team. Katie treated her helmet like a secret weapon, hiding the fact that she was a girl. If she ever saw a boy laugh or smile at her she worked even harder – hooking and blocking – to make sure they didn't get the easy day they thought they would when they realised they were marking a girl!

A hurley wasn't the only stick Katie was good with. Her PE teacher, Bridget McKeever, was an Irish hockey international and recognised that Katie had a talent for hockey, so she sent her for Ulster u16 trials. Sadly, on the day of the trial, Katie was so nervous that she didn't play well enough to make the team.

Bridget was so disappointed because she knew Katie was good enough. So, the following year she went to the trials with her. Katie played so well that she was named vice captain of the Ulster u16s. Just a few years later, Katie and Bridget were teammates, with Katie going on to make her debut for Ireland against Wales as an eighteen-year-old.

Within six years, Katie had become captain of the Irish team, leading them through a golden era for Irish women's hockey. In the summer of 2018, the team captured the hearts of the Irish nation, with the ultimate fairytale story at the World Cup in London. Ireland were one of the lowest-ranked teams in the competition, but they exceeded all expectations by reaching the World Cup final and winning the silver medal.

That medal changed everything for Irish hockey and it gave the team a new confidence when they set out on their next challenge – qualifying for the Olympics. After the heartbreak of missing out on 2012 and 2016 at the final qualification stage, Ireland won a dramatic penalty shoot-out against Canada to finally seal their place at the 2020 Tokyo Games, their first ever Olympics.

ANNALISE MURPHY

SAILING

Once there was a girl called Annalise, who sank two boats in one week, when she was only eleven years old. She grew up around boats because her mum and dad were both sailors – but keeping them afloat on her own took some time to learn!

Annalise's mum competed in the 1988 Olympics and after hearing so many stories about how amazing it was, Annalise dreamed that someday maybe she could do it too. Annalise didn't think she would be good enough, because when she started sailing, she was never the best in the class. But she loved the training and was always willing to do extra work, when everyone else had gone home.

All those extra sessions paid off when Annalise qualified for the London Olympics in 2012. She was so happy she was going to follow in her mum's footsteps and become an Olympian. Sadly, her dream had a cruel ending, when she just missed out on a medal, finishing fourth after leading the race.

Annalise cried for days. She was heartbroken, knowing how close she had come to making history for Ireland. She wanted to quit sailing and never get in a boat again but her family persuaded her to keep going. She was so glad they did and in 2013 she won a gold medal at the European Championships.

By the time Annalise went to the Olympics in Rio in 2016, she had learned so much. She knew what the heartbreak of finishing fourth felt like and she promised herself, no matter what, she wouldn't make a mistake that might cost her a medal again. So when she put herself into a medal position, she stayed calm. As she crossed the finish line in second place, she jumped into the water in celebration. This time she cried tears of joy – she had won an Olympic silver medal and in the space of four years, Annalise had turned her Olympic nightmare into a dream come true.

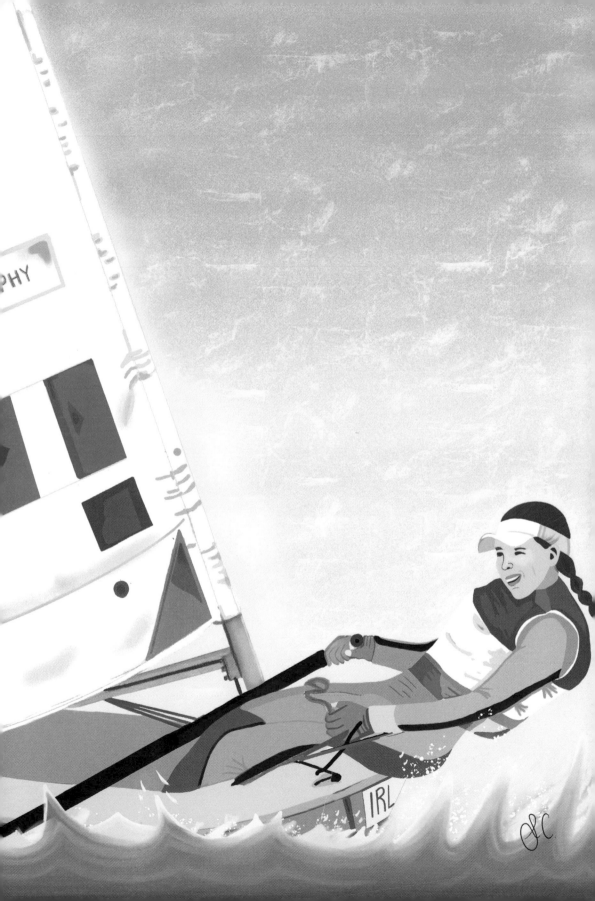

KATIE-GEORGE DUNLEVY

PARA-CYCLING

Once there was a girl called Katie, who thought she was clumsy in school because she couldn't catch a ball. It was only when doctors did some tests that they discovered Katie had a rare condition, which caused her to start losing her eyesight when she was only eleven years old.

Katie didn't want to be different and she struggled to accept help in school. So her parents decided to move her to a special school, which catered for visually impaired students. The move helped Katie to feel more confident in her own ability and she realised there were so many different sports out there that she could do, even though she was blind.

Katie's first serious sport was rowing and after initially representing Great Britain, she transferred to Ireland in the hope of making it to the 2012 Paralympics in London. She was devastated not to get picked for the team but a few weeks later she got a phone call from the Cycling Ireland National Coach, asking her to try out for the Irish para-cycling team, on a tandem (two-person) bike. Katie had never raced on a bike before but she knew she had strong legs from rowing, so she agreed to give it a try. Within a year, she was at the Paralympics – as a cyclist!

At the 2016 Paralympics, Katie had a new partner for the tandem, Eve McCrystal, a triathlete looking for a new challenge. Katie put her trust in Eve and together they won two medals – a gold and a silver.

Over the next three years they took the para-cycling world by storm, as they became triple world champions. When they returned to the Paralympics in 2021, they surpassed even their own expectations, with two golds and a silver, to become one of the most successful duos to ever represent Ireland.

Natalya Coyle

MODERN PENTATHLON

Once there was a girl called Natalya, who was good at lots of sports but really hated to lose. She still remembers the day, in senior infants, that she lost in the egg and spoon race. She was so upset that her mum had to come and collect her from school. Natalya cried all the way home but her mum told her to remember that even if you lose one race, you can still win the next one.

School Sports Day was Natalya's favourite day of the year. She loved the variety of doing lots of different sports. So when she was introduced to the pentathlon as a teenager, she thought it would be a great challenge – five different sports (running, shooting, fencing, swimming and showjumping) and five chances to win!

Natalya first represented Ireland when she was seventeen and she surprised even herself when she qualified for the Olympics just three years later. Ireland had never had a female modern pentathlete at the Olympics before, so going to London in 2012 was like a dream come true. Natalya knew she was one of the youngest athletes but she surprised herself again with a brilliant ninth-place finish.

Four years later, Natalya went back to the Olympics, in Brazil, with more expectation on her shoulders. This time, Natalya wasn't surprising anyone. Her rivals knew she had a big chance and she came close to winning a medal, battling bravely to finish sixth. Afterwards, Natalya thought life couldn't get any better. Two top ten finishes at the Olympics was more than she could ever have imagined.

Natalya knew, with the progress she was making, winning a world medal wasn't far away and two years later she finally stood on the podium, as she won a Modern Pentathlon World Cup silver medal. Just like School Sports Day, she didn't win every race, but when it mattered most, Natalya gave it her all and achieved what was Ireland's best ever finish at a World Cup event.

Natalya Coyle

NICCI DALY

HOCKEY & MOTORSPORT

Once there was a girl called Nicci, who dreamed of being a racing car driver, just like her dad, who raced in Formula Ford. Nicci begged him to let her race a go-kart and she won her first competition when she was only eleven years old. Sadly, Nicci's dad passed away when she was just fourteen and after that she found it hard to race without him.

When Nicci first started playing hockey, she hated it and wanted to quit. She preferred Gaelic football and she was enjoying playing on the Dublin u14 team. Her mum convinced her to keep playing hockey and Nicci was glad she listened to her when she made the Irish u18 squad in her Leaving Cert year.

Nicci's sporting career reached a crossroads in 2009, when she was called up to the Dublin senior football squad and the Irish hockey team at the same time. While the Dublin footballers were close to making a breakthrough, the opportunity to play for her country was too hard to turn down.

Nicci's commitment to the hockey team was rewarded in the summer of 2018, when she helped Ireland to win a World Cup silver medal. Reaching the World Cup final felt like Christmas had come early for the team, so they started singing Mariah Carey's 'All I Want for Christmas', in the middle of July, in London. It drew so much attention that Mariah Carey herself tweeted about it!

A year later, Nicci scored a penalty in a dramatic shoot-out against Canada, as the Irish team qualified for their first ever Olympic Games.

Nicci never lost her love of motorsport, even though her sporting career took her in a different direction. In 2018, she set up a female racing team called Formula Female and thanks to her, a new generation of young girls can now follow that dream of becoming a racing car driver – just like she did.

SARAH ROWE

Once there was a girl called Sarah, who was chosen to play in Croke Park at half-time during the 2007 ladies football final, after impressing for her team in a Cumann na mBunscol final.

Just a few years later, Sarah was no longer the half-time entertainment, she was a Mayo player. She was training with girls she looked up to and it really was a dream come true. But Gaelic football wasn't Sarah's only sport. She was also very good at soccer and she was picked for the Irish u15 team around the same time.

Sarah tried her best to juggle both sports. During her Leaving Cert year, she played for the Republic of Ireland u19s as they reached the semi-finals of the European Championships. Two weeks later, she was player of the match as Mayo reached the quarter-finals of the Ladies Football Championship.

Sarah made her debut for the Republic of Ireland senior squad the following summer, but she found it hard to balance everything. So she chose to put her focus solely on Gaelic football for a few years.

In 2018, another opportunity came along, as she was offered the chance to play Aussie Rules. Sarah had always loved the idea of being a professional athlete but she didn't want to stop playing for Mayo. Luckily, the LGFA (Ladies Gaelic Football Association) and Aussie Rules seasons are played at different times of the year, which means Sarah can play Aussie Rules for the first few months of the year and play with Mayo during the summer.

Sarah's first season with her club, Collingwood, was such a success, she was awarded the AFLW's (Australian Football League Women's) Multicultural Player of the Year award, for players in the league born outside of Australia. Sarah had made her mark at the highest level in yet another sport and after years of trying to find a balance, she finally had the best of both worlds!

Sarah Rowe

DERVAL O'ROURKE

HURDLES

Once there was a girl called Derval, who believed she was the fastest child on her road. She told all the other kids she would beat them in a race but they laughed, because she was the youngest. One day, an older boy called Billy said he would race her to the wall at the end of their estate. Derval ran with all her might and beat him, but she was running so fast that she couldn't stop and she cut her knees off the concrete wall. It hurt so much that Billy had to help her home. Even through the pain, she slept well that night knowing she had won the race!

Derval took up athletics when she was in school and she also played hockey and gymnastics, but none of them fascinated her like running. She loved how she could time herself one day and then try to beat that time the next day. She started off as a sprinter but moved to hurdles when she realised she could win more races. Derval became obsessed with beating her own records ... and she set lots of them!

Derval set her first national record in the 100m hurdles at the European u23 Athletics Championships in 2003 and she knew she was making big progress because of her improving times. Three years later, she was the youngest girl in the race when she stepped onto the track in Moscow, at the World Indoor Championships. She thought of Billy and the kids in her estate, who laughed when she said she was the fastest. She put her head down and started sprinting and jumping over the hurdles as fast as she could. In less than eight seconds, Derval's life changed, as she became World Indoor champion in the 60m hurdles.

That was one of five major medals Derval won at European and World Championships and she also represented Ireland at three Olympic Games. Derval's confidence in her own ability is what made her one of Ireland's best ever championship performers.

JOY NEVILLE

Once there was a girl called Joy, who grew up in Limerick in a sports-mad household. Her first introduction to rugby was in the backyard with her four older brothers. They didn't care that she was a girl or that she was the youngest. They were just as rough with her as they were with each other, and Joy loved that.

One day, she got an accidental shoulder into the face and broke her nose. She knew if she told her parents they wouldn't let her play anymore, so she hid outside for a few hours instead.

That toughness was one of Joy's trademark qualities. When she started playing rugby properly at seventeen, she was immediately recognised as a bright talent and she made her Irish debut within three years. She went on to captain Ireland, leading the team to their first ever win against France in the Six Nations in 2009, with her brothers sitting proudly in the stands. Four years later, Joy was one of the star players as Ireland won a first ever Grand Slam title in 2013.

After winning the Grand Slam, Joy retired from playing rugby and was asked if she would consider becoming a referee. She laughed, saying, 'Sure, I didn't even know half the rules when I was playing!' She gave it a try and for the first few months she hated it and wanted to quit, but her family and friends convinced her to keep going, because they knew she had huge potential.

It wasn't easy and there were people who thought a woman couldn't referee a game of men's rugby. In 2016, Joy proved them wrong, as she became the first woman to referee a professional men's European rugby match. A rapid rise through the ranks saw Joy named World Rugby Referee of the Year in 2017 and she continues to be one of the world's leading referees to this day.

BRIEGE CORKERY

CAMOGIE & LADIES FOOTBALL

Once there was a girl called Briege, who had short hair and was never afraid to get stuck in when playing with the boys. One day she was playing in a school football match and every time she picked the ball up straight off the ground, the referee gave a free against her. It was only when Briege's teacher ran in to say that girls were allowed to pick the ball up off the ground, that the referee realised his mistake – he thought that Briege was a boy!

Briege played with the Cork u14 footballers for two years, but after that she didn't make the minor panel. She was devastated. Later that year, the senior footballers were short players for a league game against Dublin, so they asked Briege to play. She laughed to herself because she couldn't even make the minor panel but she was making her debut for the seniors, as a fifteen-year-old!

Briege was also a talented camogie player and she was called up to the Cork senior panel when she was seventeen. She never wanted to choose between the two sports but there were some times when big matches were fixed for the same weekend and Briege had to play one or the other. Or sometimes both.

Briege had so many amazing days in Croke Park. In 2014, she was the captain when the Cork ladies footballers made one of the most memorable comebacks in Irish sporting history. Cork were losing to Dublin by ten points with fifteen minutes to go in the All-Ireland final but Briege and her teammates never gave up and somehow they fought back to win the game by one point. She knew she wouldn't forget that day for the rest of her life!

Briege never played sport to win medals. Yet, between 2005 and 2018, she won a record eighteen All-Ireland medals and sixteen All-Stars. Her last All-Ireland with the Cork camogie team was extra special, because her five-month-old son Tadhg was there in the stands.

CIARA MAGEEAN

ATHLETICS

Once there was a girl called Ciara, who dreamed of playing camogie for Down. Her dad played hurling for Down and her aunt had also represented Down and Antrim in camogie. When Ciara made the Down minor camogie team, she thought it was the beginning of a long career in the red and black jersey. What she didn't realise was that her teacher had also spotted her natural ability to run.

Ciara was only eleven years old when she ran her first race. Halfway through she got tired and started walking. When she started running again, she caught up to the leaders and managed to finish fourth. She was so angry with herself for stopping, she vowed she would never give up during a race again.

That fighting spirit is something Ciara has become known for in her athletics career. She was only seventeen when she won her first major medal, at the World Youth Championships in 2009. A year later, she finished in the top ten of the women's 1500m at the Commonwealth Games, in her first senior competition.

Ciara never lost her love for camogie. Sometimes she would even sneak out to play matches when she was supposed to be resting after athletics training. One day, as she was coming back into the house, her dad asked her, 'How was the match?' Ciara smiled and tried to lie, saying she wasn't at any match. Her dad laughed back, telling her he was there too and saw her playing!

Ciara soon focused on running and her dedication paid off when she won a medal at the European Championships in 2016, becoming only the third Irish woman to do so. She won another medal in 2019 at the European Indoors and finished tenth at the World Championships.

A dream season in 2022 saw Ciara win silver medals at the European Championships and the Commonwealth Games. She then won a prestigious Diamond League race against some of the world's top athletes, breaking Sonia O'Sullivan's 27-year Irish record in the process. As she says herself, 'Not bad for a wee girl from Portaferry!'

RISING

Tyler Toland ★ Soccer

Tyler became the youngest ever player to be capped for the Republic of Ireland, making her senior debut just a month after her sixteenth birthday. She now plays for Manchester City in the Women's Super League in England.

Gina Akpe-Moses ★ Athletics

Gina was a talented sprinter from a young age, winning her first major medal at the European Youth Olympics in 2015. When she was eighteen, she won a gold medal in the 100m race at the European u20 Championships.

Lara Gillespie ★ Cycling

Lara won a silver medal at the European Youth Olympics in 2017 and became a European junior champion a year later. In 2019, she wrote herself into the history books, winning Ireland's first ever medal at the World Junior Track Championships, when she won a bronze in the individual pursuit race.

STARS

Mona McSharry ★ Swimming

Mona became a junior world champion in 2017, the first ever Irish person to do so. She broke four Irish records in three days during her first senior year of competition and won a bronze medal at the European Short Course Championships in 2019.

Saoirse Noonan ★ GAA/Soccer

Saoirse is a multi-talented athlete. She made her debut for the Cork senior footballers in 2018 as a teenager, while also playing soccer for Cork City and the Republic of Ireland u19s. She continues to play soccer and gaelic football at the highest level in Ireland.

Beibhinn Parsons ★ Rugby

Beibhinn made her debut as a sixteen-year-old in 2018, making her the youngest ever player capped for the Irish rugby team. She has quickly become one of the brightest stars in the game, as a regular face on the Irish 15s and 7s rugby teams.